GREAT -»BOOKISH« QUOTES

WORDS FROM *authors, libraries,* AND *books* THAT SHAPED THE WORLD

ALA American Library Associatior

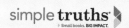
simple truths®
ˌ Small books. **BIG IMPACT.**

Published by Sourcebooks
P.O. Box 4410, Naperville, Illinois 60567-4410
(630) 961-3900
sourcebooks.com

Printed and bound in China.
PP 10 9 8 7 6 5 4 3 2 1

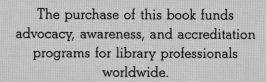

The purchase of this book funds advocacy, awareness, and accreditation programs for library professionals worldwide.

FOR LIBRARY LOVERS
everywhere.

DEAR LIBRARY LOVER,

A good quote is a chance to hear a new perspective, to spur new ideas, or to affirm what we already know is true. Quotes can also be a welcome pick-me-up that remotivates you to do the work you do every day.

Within these pages you'll find some of our favorite quotes about libraries and the library life from today's writers and thinkers. They celebrate the many ways library lovers champion democracy, protect intellectual freedom, promote knowledge, and provide a safe haven for the human spirit.

We hope this collection will surprise you, excite you, and uplift you. ARE YOU READY TO BE INSPIRED?

—Your friends at the American Library Association

A LIBRARY IN THE MIDDLE
OF A COMMUNITY IS A CROSS
BETWEEN AN EMERGENCY EXIT, A LIFE
RAFT, AND A FESTIVAL. THEY ARE
CATHEDRALS OF THE MIND; HOSPITALS
OF THE SOUL; THEME PARKS OF
THE IMAGINATION.

—CAITLIN MORAN

BOOK

A library is a *temple* unabridged

with priceless treasure. Librarians are

the *majesties* who loan the jewels of measure.

They welcome to the kingdom the young and old

of reapers and reign among the riches as

the wondrous *fortune keepers.*

—PAM MUÑOZ RYAN

A LIBRARY
IS INFINITY
UNDER A
ROOF.

—GAIL CARSON LEVINE

Reading is the key that opens doors to many good things in life. Reading shaped my dreams, and more reading helped me make my dreams come true.

—RUTH BADER GINSBURG

CENSORSHIP
IS TO ART AS LYNCHING IS TO JUSTICE.

—HENRY LOUIS GATES JR.

Walking the *stacks* in a library, dragging your fingers across the *spines*—it's hard not to feel the presence of *sleeping spirits.*

—ROBIN SLOAN

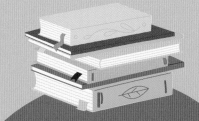

SOMEDAY I WILL STOP BEING SURPRISED
AT ALL THE THINGS LIBRARIANS READ;
THEY'LL READ ANYTHING.

—MARILYN JOHNSON

LIBRARIES
ALWAYS REMIND ME
THAT THERE ARE
good things
in this world.

—LAUREN WARD

Banning books gives us **silence** when we need speech. It closes our ears when we need to **listen**. It makes us blind when we need **sight**.

—STEPHEN CHBOSKY

TO A HISTORIAN, LIBRARIES ARE FOOD, SHELTER, AND EVEN MUSE.

—BARBARA W. TUCHMAN

The library is the **temple of learning,**
and learning has **liberated** more people
than all the wars in **history.**

—CARL T. ROWAN

WHEN I DISCOVERED LIBRARIES, IT WAS LIKE HAVING CHRISTMAS EVERY DAY.

—JEAN FRITZ

The pursuit of knowing was *freedom* to me, the right to declare your own *curiosities* and follow them through all manner of books. I was made for the library, not the classroom. The *classroom* was a jail of other people's interests. The library was open, unending, free. Slowly, I was *discovering myself.*

—TA-NEHISI COATES

LIBRARIES ARE THE ULTIMATE
RESTAURANTS FOR BRAIN FOOD.
I SLEEP BETTER KNOWING
THERE ARE LIBRARIES.
I WOULD TAKE A BULLET
FOR A LIBRARIAN.

—SIMON VAN BOOY

I'VE READ
TOO MANY BOOKS
TO BELIEVE WHAT
I AM TOLD.

—SUHEIR HAMMAD

Civilized nations build libraries;
lands that have lost their soul
close them down.

—TOBY FORWARD

Most people don't understand what a library does for me, and I've tried to explain it to them. All I know is that I feel energized when I'm in one. My pulse quickens when I walk through the stacks. I feel like an explorer surveying an uncharted shore. Lost worlds are here waiting to be discovered. Ancient worlds; once glorious, not crumbled. Future worlds; no more substantial than the numbers or ideas or words of those who dream them. Mythical worlds. Worlds of limitless dimensions. Libraries are medieval forests masking opportunity and danger; every aisle is a path, every catalog reference a clue to the location of the Holy Grail.

—JACK CAVANAUGH

What is freedom of expression?

Without the freedom to offend,

it ceases to exist.

—SALMAN RUSHDIE

LIBRARIES ARE THE THIN RED LINE BETWEEN CIVILIZATION AND BARBARISM.

—NEIL GAIMAN

There are certain *emotions* in your body that
not even your best friend can sympathize with,
but you will find the *right film* or the
right book, and it will understand you.

—BJÖRK GUÐMUNDSDÓTTIR

WHEN I WAS YOUNG,
WE COULDN'T AFFORD MUCH.
BUT, MY LIBRARY CARD WAS MY
KEY TO THE WORLD.

—JOHN GOODMAN

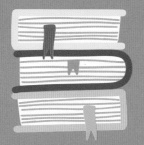

LIBRARIES ARE EVERYMAN'S FREE UNIVERSITY.

—JOHN JAKES

THE LIBRARY IS AN ARENA OF POSSIBILITY, OPENING BOTH A WINDOW INTO THE SOUL AND A DOOR ONTO THE WORLD.

—RITA DOVE

Libraries store the energy that fuels the imagination. They open up windows to the world and inspire us to explore and achieve, and contribute to improving our quality of life. Libraries change lives for the better.

—SIDNEY SHELDON

[Librarians] are subversive.
You think they're just sitting there at
the desk, all quiet and everything.
They're like plotting the revolution, man.
I wouldn't mess with them.

—MICHAEL MOORE

I ALWAYS FELT,
IN ANY TOWN,
IF I CAN GET
TO A LIBRARY,
I'LL BE OKAY.

—MAYA ANGELOU

A public library is the most

democratic thing in the world.

What can be found there has

undone dictators and tyrants.

—DORIS LESSING

IF YOU ONLY READ THE BOOKS
THAT EVERYONE ELSE IS READING,
YOU CAN ONLY THINK WHAT
EVERYONE ELSE IS THINKING.

—HARUKI MURAKAMI

When you are **growing up**, there are two institutional places that **affect** you most powerfully: the **church**, which belongs to God, and the **public library**, which belongs to you. The public library is a **great equalizer**.

—KEITH RICHARDS

A TRULY GREAT LIBRARY

CONTAINS SOMETHING IN IT

TO OFFEND EVERYONE.

—MARY JO GODWIN

LEARNING

is the key to

LIBERATION

—ALICE WALKER

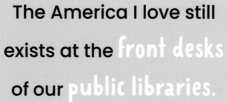

The America I love still exists at the **front desks** of our **public libraries.**

—KURT VONNEGUT

The story is truly **finished**—and meaning is made—not when the author adds the **last period**, but when the **reader enters**.

—CELESTE NG

The public library
is where place and
possibility meet.

—STUART DYBEK

A book, too, can be a star, explosive material, capable of stirring up fresh life endlessly, a living fire to lighten the darkness, leading out into the expanding universe.

—MADELEINE L'ENGLE

WE READ TO KNOW THAT WE ARE NOT ALONE.

—WILLIAM NICHOLSON

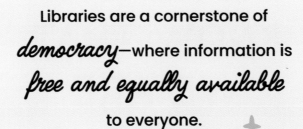

Libraries are a cornerstone of

democracy—where information is

free and equally available

to everyone.

—CARLA HAYDEN

Knowledge and information—and by which I do very much include the internet—**is a forest.** And true, sometimes it's fun getting lost, sometimes that's how you learn some **surprising things.** But how much more can you discover when someone can point you in the right direction, when someone can maybe give you **a map.** When someone can maybe even give you a treasure map, to **places** you may not have even thought you were allowed to go. *This is what librarians do.*

—PATRICK NESS

In the nonstop tsunami of global information, librarians provide us with floaties and **teach us to swim.**

—LINTON WEEKS

BOOKS TRAIN YOUR IMAGINATION TO THINK BIG.

—TAYLOR SWIFT

PEOPLE CAN LOSE THEIR
LIVES IN LIBRARIES.
THEY OUGHT TO
BE WARNED.

—SAUL BELLOW

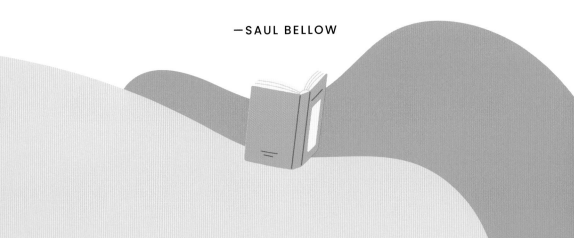

I love librarians. I think the whole idea of being a librarian is extraordinary. Not only that you live your life with books and for books but that you can guide a young reader. That's so important.

—ISABEL ALLENDE

WHAT I LOVE MOST ABOUT READING: IT GIVES YOU THE ABILITY TO REACH HIGHER GROUND. AND KEEP CLIMBING.

—OPRAH WINFREY

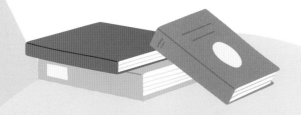

A library is the only
single place you can go to
learn something new,
be comforted, terrified,
thrilled, saddened,
overjoyed, or excited
all in one day.
And for free.

—AMY NEFTZGER

Librarians hoard the *wisdom* of humanity. They are the *keepers* of all knowledge, the *guardians* at the temples of understanding and *devoted protectors* of the sanctuary in the midst of uneducated anarchy.

—STEPHEN COLBERT

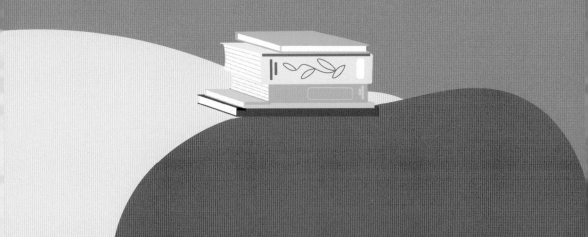

ALL KNOWLEDGE IS CONNECTED TO
ALL OTHER KNOWLEDGE. THE FUN
IS IN MAKING THE CONNECTIONS.

—ARTHUR AUFDERHEIDE

You think your *pain* and your *heartbreak* are unprecedented in the history of the world, but then you read. It was *books* that taught me that the things that tormented me most were the very things that *connected* me with all the people who were alive, or who had ever been *alive.*

—JAMES BALDWIN

IN TIMES OF TROUBLE,
LIBRARIES ARE SANCTUARIES.

—SUSAN ORLEAN

I wouldn't be a *songwriter* if it wasn't for *books* that I loved as a kid. I think that when you can *escape* into a book, it trains your *imagination* to think big and to think that more can *exist* than what you see.

—TAYLOR SWIFT

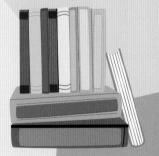

Libraries represent the diversity and immensity of human thought, our collective knowledge laid out in rows of revealing inspiration.

—MANUEL LIMA

NEVER ARGUE WITH A LIBRARIAN; THEY KNOW TOO MUCH.

—CAROLE NELSON DOUGLAS

A library is a house of *hope*.
It's a *place* where we all,
whatever our situation,
can feed our *ideas* and
develop our *dreams*.

—DOUG WILHELM

If you're really in favor of *free speech,* then you're in favor of freedom of speech for *precisely* the views you *despise.* Otherwise, you're not in *favor* of free speech.

—NOAM CHOMSKY

THE LIBRARY IS LIKE
A CANDY STORE WHERE
EVERYTHING IS FREE.

—JAMIE FORD

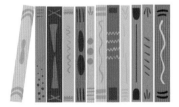

ONE CHILD, ONE TEACHER, ONE BOOK, ONE PEN

can change the world.

—MALALA YOUSAFZAI

Libraries really are wonderful. They're better than bookshops, even. I mean bookshops make a profit on selling you books, but libraries just sit there lending you books quietly out of the goodness of their hearts.

—JO WALTON

I'M OF A FEARSOME MIND TO
THROW MY ARMS AROUND EVERY
LIVING LIBRARIAN WHO CROSSES MY
PATH, ON BEHALF OF THE SOULS THEY
NEVER KNEW THEY SAVED.

—BARBARA KINGSOLVER

A great library doesn't have to be *big* or *beautiful.* It doesn't have to have the best facilities or the most efficient staff or the most users. A great library *provides.* It is enmeshed in the life of a *community* in a way that makes it indispensable.

—VICKI MYRON

I look at books
as being a form of activism.
Sometimes they'll show us a
side of the world that we might
not have known about.

—ANGIE THOMAS

The truth is libraries are raucous *clubhouses* for free speech, controversy, and community. Librarians have *stood up* to the Patriot Act, *sat down* with noisy toddlers, and *reached out* to illiterate adults. Libraries can never be shushed.

—PAULA POUNDSTONE

THE CURRENT DEFINITIVE ANSWER

TO ALMOST ANY QUESTION CAN BE

FOUND WITHIN THE FOUR WALLS

OF MOST LIBRARIES.

—ARTHUR ASHE

Stories have given me a place in which to lose myself. They have allowed me to **remember**. They have allowed me to **forget**. They have allowed me to imagine different **endings** and better possible **worlds**.

—ROXANE GAY

LIBRARIES ARE THE BEATING HEARTS OF OUR COMMUNITIES.

—EMILIO ESTEVEZ

Access to knowledge is the *superb,*

the supreme act of *truly* great civilizations.

Of all the institutions that purport to do this,

free libraries stand *virtually* alone in

accomplishing this mission.

—TONI MORRISON

IF I HAD MY DRUTHERS,
I WOULD BE BURIED IN A LIBRARY OR
INSIDE A COFFIN THAT RESEMBLED ONE—
THAT'S HOW I FEEL ABOUT THEM.

—JUNOT DÍAZ

A library is a focal point, a sacred place to a community; and its sacredness is its accessibility, its publicness. It's everybody's place.

—URSULA K. LE GUIN

It's not merely that
libraries connect us to books.
It's that they connect us
to one another.

—CHRIS BOHJALIAN

Maybe this is *why we read,* and why in moments of darkness we *return to books:* to find *words* for what we already know.

—ALBERTO MANGUEL

The library card is a passport to *wonders and miracles*, glimpses into other lives, religions, experiences, the *hopes* and *dreams* and *strivings* of ALL human beings, and it is this passport that opens our *eyes and hearts* to the world beyond our front doors, that is one of our *best hopes* against tyranny, xenophobia, hopelessness, despair, anarchy, and ignorance.

—LIBBA BRAY

A BOOK IS A

WHOLE WORLD THAT

YOU CAN FIT INTO

YOUR POCKET.

—MATSHONA DHLIWAYO

To ask why we need libraries at all, when there is so much **information** available elsewhere, is about as sensible as asking if **roadmaps** are necessary now that there are so very many **roads**.

—JON BING

WHEN I READ A DARING BOOK
OR LISTEN TO REBELLIOUS MUSIC,
I FEEL LIKE I'VE FOUND WHAT
FREEDOM REALLY MEANS.

—CARLA H. KRUEGER

The message is clear: *libraries matter.*
Their solid presence at the heart of
our towns sends the *proud signal* that
everyone—whoever they are, whatever
their educational background, whatever their
age or their needs—*is welcome.*

—KATE MOSSE

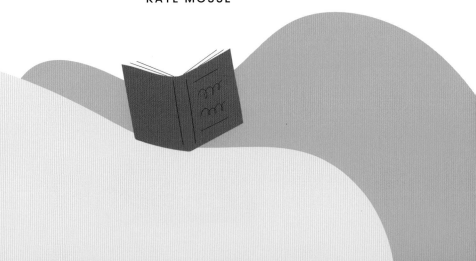

Books have given me a magic portal
to connect with people of the past and
the present. I know I shall never feel
lonely or powerless again.

—LISA BU

LIBRARIANS ARE AT THE HEART
OF OPPOSITION TO FOOLISH,
DANGEROUS, MISGUIDED ATTEMPTS
AT CENSORING HUMAN EXPRESSION
IN OUR FREE COUNTRY.

—CLYDE EDGERTON

Well-run libraries are filled with people because what a good library offers cannot be easily found elsewhere: an indoor public space in which you do not have to buy anything in order to stay.

—ZADIE SMITH

BOOKS ARE THE
PLANE, AND THE TRAIN,
AND THE ROAD. THEY
ARE THE DESTINATION,
AND THE JOURNEY.
THEY ARE HOME.

—ANNA QUINDLEN

For me, libraries are the great **equalizer.** Everybody goes into the library, whether they're **powerful** or not, whether they're **rich** or not, and they realize, man, there is so much out there. We're so **little** compared to all that there is in this time and place that we live. I like that **dimension** of libraries.

—RICK STEVES

I AM PART OF EVERYTHING THAT I HAVE READ.

—THEODORE ROOSEVELT

In big cities and small towns, libraries *fulfill* a purpose that almost nothing else does. They're a *place* of information for all. A place where people can come *together* as a community.

—JILL BIDEN

I have always thought that librarians are a little bit like doctors, travel agents, and professors all rolled into one. We all know that a great story can lift spirits, take you anywhere in the world you want to go and in any time period to boot, and the lessons you learn from a good book can buoy your own convictions and even change your life.

—DOROTHEA BENTON FRANK

[THE LIBRARY IS]
MORE THAN A PLACE OF
BOOKS—IT'S A PLACE OF
SOLACE AND REST AND
REGENERATION, A VERY
WONDERFUL PLACE.

—ZIGGY MARLEY

FEW THINGS ARE BETTER
IN THE WORLD THAN A
ROOM FULL OF LIBRARIANS.
I CONSIDER THEM LITERARY
HEROES. THE KEEPERS
AND DEFENDERS OF THE
WRITTEN WORD.

—LOUISE PENNY

YOU CAN NEVER GET A CUP OF TEA LARGE ENOUGH OR A BOOK LONG ENOUGH TO SUIT ME.

—C. S. LEWIS

LIBRARIANS
HAVE KNOWLEDGE.
THEY GUIDE YOU
TO THE RIGHT BOOKS.
THE RIGHT WORLDS.
THEY FIND THE BEST
PLACES. LIKE SOUL-
ENHANCED SEARCH
ENGINES.

—MATT HAIG

[W]hat people truly desire is **access** to the knowledge and information that ultimately lead to a **better life**—the collected wisdom of the ages found only in one **place**: a well-stocked library.

—LINDA SUE PARK

LIBRARIANS...PUT THEIR HEARTS
AND MINDS INTO PRESERVING
KNOWLEDGE AND MAKING IT
AVAILABLE TO ALL. THEY HELP TO KEEP
THE WHEELS OF TRUTH, DISCOVERY,
AND IMAGINATION TURNING.

—L. J. M. OWEN

Let's stop thinking of libraries as *austere* study spaces, as *quiet places* where books gather dust, and instead think of them as the vital *heart* of a healthy society, as social enablers, as *safe spaces* for marginalized groups and a place of discovery, because at their best, a library can be *anything* you need it to be, *anything* you want, *anything* at all.

—MAARYA REHMAN

Every book, every **volume** you see here, has a soul. The soul of the **person** who wrote it and of those who read it and **lived** and **dreamed** with it. Every time a book changes hands, every time someone runs his **eyes** down its pages, its spirit **grows** and **strengthens**.

—CARLOS RUIZ ZAFÓN

READING IS THE SOLE MEANS
BY WHICH WE SLIP, INVOLUNTARILY,
OFTEN HELPLESSLY, INTO ANOTHER'S
SKIN, ANOTHER'S VOICE,
ANOTHER'S SOUL.

—JOYCE CAROL OATES

More than a *building* that houses books and data, the library represents a *window* to a larger world, the place where we've always come to discover big *ideas* and profound *concepts* that help move the *American* story forward and the *human* story forward.

—BARACK OBAMA

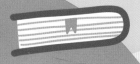

PEOPLE ARE HUNGRY FOR STORIES.

IT'S PART OF OUR VERY BEING.

STORYTELLING IS A FORM OF HISTORY,

OF IMMORTALITY, TOO. IT GOES FROM

ONE GENERATION TO ANOTHER.

—STUDS TERKEL

The role of a librarian is to make sense of the world of information. If that's not a qualification for superhero-dom, what is?

—NANCY PEARL

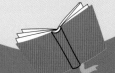

Libraries, as spaces, need to *continue* to *inspire* the public to dream big and to think great *thoughts.* Cities, towns, and academic communities of all *shapes* and *sizes* need the free, open public spaces that libraries—and only libraries—provide.

—JOHN PALFREY

BOOKS UNITE US.

CENSORSHIP DIVIDES US.

—JASON REYNOLDS

I LIKE LIBRARIES. IT MAKES ME FEEL COMFORTABLE AND SECURE TO HAVE WALLS OF WORDS, BEAUTIFUL AND WISE, ALL AROUND ME. I ALWAYS FEEL BETTER WHEN I CAN SEE THAT THERE IS SOMETHING TO HOLD BACK THE SHADOWS.

—ROGER ZELAZNY

UNTIL I BECAME
A LIBRARIAN,
I DIDN'T KNOW
I WAS A REBEL.

—ALECHIA DOW

Libraries are reservoirs of *strength,*
grace and *wit,* reminders of *order,*
calm and *continuity,* lakes of mental
energy, neither *warm* nor *cold,*
light nor *dark.*

—GERMAINE GREER

THE SEEDS OF DREAMS ARE OFTEN

FOUND IN BOOKS, AND THE SEEDS YOU HELP

PLANT IN YOUR COMMUNITY CAN GROW

ACROSS THE WORLD.

—DOLLY PARTON

LIBRARIES ARE...
TO CIVILIZATION...
WHAT WATER IS
TO FISH.

—AYAAN HIRSI ALI

Libraries have a transformative effect on lives of all ages, the communities in which they reside, and the country as a whole. They were, and still are, civic institutions that welcome anyone who wishes to become a more informed and independent citizen. There is no other public resource that so well encapsulates this aspirational notion of democracy. Through the library, through books, through knowledge, through access to technology, we all can improve to become better, more learned, versions of ourselves and, in turn, be better neighbors to those around us.

—DAN RATHER

ANYONE WHO SAYS THEY HAVE
ONLY ONE LIFE TO LIVE MUST NOT
KNOW HOW TO READ A BOOK.

—UNKNOWN

A LIBRARY SHOULD BE LIKE A PAIR OF OPEN ARMS.

—ROGER ROSENBLATT

Public libraries are the
heart and soul of any community.
They are a place to read and think
and browse and dream.

—MARY McNEAR

[LIBRARIANS] HAVE THE POWER
TO EXPAND PEOPLE'S PERSPECTIVES,
AND THAT'S THE NUMBER ONE
THING WE NEED TO DO RIGHT NOW.

—W. KAMAU BELL

Thank you for standing up for libraries, for open *minds,* for free and unfettered *access* to information. It *matters* so much for so many.

—MARGARET ATWOOD

GOOD FRIENDS,
GOOD BOOKS,

AND A SLEEPY
CONSCIENCE:

THIS IS THE
IDEAL LIFE.

—MARK TWAIN

People think librarians are unromantic, unimaginative. *This is not true.* We are people whose dreams run in particular ways. Ask a mountain climber what he *feels* when he sees a mountain; a lion tamer what goes through his *mind* when he meets a new lion; a doctor confronted with a *beautiful* malfunctioning body. The idea of a library full of books, the books full of knowledge, fills me with *fear* and *love* and *courage* and endless *wonder.*

—ELIZABETH McCRACKEN

She reads books as
one would breathe air,
to fill up and **LIVE.**

—ANNE DILLARD

It is what you *read* when you don't have to that *determines* what you will be when you *can't* help it.

—OSCAR WILDE

Do not, under any circumstances, belittle a work of fiction by trying to turn it into a carbon copy of real life; what we search for in fiction is not so much reality but the epiphany of truth.

—AZAR NAFISI

THERE IS NO FRIEND AS LOYAL AS A BOOK.

—ERNEST HEMINGWAY

THERE IS MORE TREASURE
IN BOOKS THAN IN ALL
THE PIRATE'S LOOT ON
TREASURE ISLAND.

—WALT DISNEY

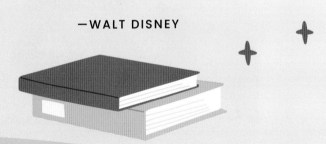

After nourishment, shelter and companionship, stories are the thing we need most in the world.

—PHILIP PULLMAN

One of the joys of *reading* is the ability to plug into the shared *wisdom* of mankind.

—ISHMAEL REED

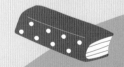

THE MORE THAT YOU READ,

THE MORE THINGS YOU WILL KNOW.

THE MORE THAT YOU LEARN,

THE MORE PLACES YOU'LL GO.

—DR. SEUSS

BOOKS HAVE TO BE HEAVY

BECAUSE THE WHOLE WORLD'S INSIDE THEM.

—CORNELIA FUNKE

Many a book is like a key to unknown chambers within the castle of one's own self.

—FRANZ KAFKA

BOOKS ARE A UNIQUELY PORTABLE MAGIC.

—STEPHEN KING

ONE MUST ALWAYS BE CAREFUL

OF BOOKS AND WHAT IS INSIDE THEM,

FOR WORDS HAVE THE POWER

TO CHANGE US.

—CASSANDRA CLARE

A GOOD BOOK IS NEVER EXHAUSTED.
IT GOES ON WHISPERING TO YOU
FROM THE WALL.

—ANATOLE BROYARD

OPEN BOOKS LEAD TO OPEN MINDS.

—UNKNOWN

IF A BOOK IS WELL WRITTEN,
I always find it too short.

—JANE AUSTEN

Some books are so familiar that reading them is like being home again.

—LOUISA MAY ALCOTT

I LIVED IN BOOKS MORE THAN I LIVED ANYWHERE ELSE.

—NEIL GAIMAN

Where is human nature so weak as in the bookstore?

—HENRY WARD BEECHER

I READ A BOOK ONE DAY AND MY WHOLE LIFE WAS CHANGED.

—ORHAN PAMUK

THE ONLY THING THAT YOU
ABSOLUTELY HAVE TO KNOW IS
THE LOCATION OF THE LIBRARY.

—ALBERT EINSTEIN

I love the *sound* of the pages *flicking* against my fingers. Print against *fingerprints.* Books make people *quiet,* yet they are *so loud.*

—NNEDI OKORAFOR

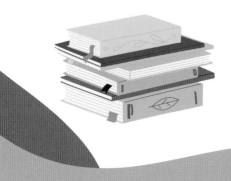

There is no mistaking a
real book when one meets it.
It is like falling in love.

—CHRISTOPHER MORLEY

Books are the **quietest** and most **constant** of friends; they are the most **accessible** and **wisest** of counsellors, and the most **patient** of teachers.

—CHARLES WILLIAM ELIOT

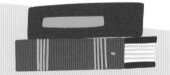

READING IS LIKE THINKING, LIKE PRAYING, LIKE TALKING TO A FRIEND, LIKE EXPRESSING YOUR IDEAS, LIKE LISTENING TO OTHER PEOPLE'S IDEAS, LIKE LISTENING TO MUSIC, LIKE LOOKING AT THE VIEW, LIKE TAKING A WALK ON THE BEACH.

—ROBERTO BOLAÑO

IN THE END, WE ALL BECOME STORIES.

—MARGARET ATWOOD

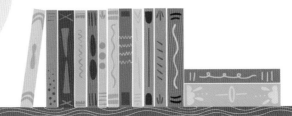

quoted
FOLKS

LOUISA MAY ALCOTT (1832–1888) was an American novelist, short story writer, and poet best known as the author of the novel *Little Women*.

ISABEL ALLENDE (1942–) is a Chilean writer best known for novels *The House of the Spirits* and *City of the Beasts*.

MAYA ANGELOU (1928–2014) was an American poet, memoirist, and civil rights activist.

ARTHUR ASHE (1943–1993) was an American professional tennis player who won three Grand Slam singles titles.

MARGARET ATWOOD (1939–) is a Canadian poet, novelist, literary critic, essayist, teacher, environmental activist, and inventor.

ARTHUR AUFDERHEIDE (1922–2013) was an American pathologist who pioneered the study of diseases in ancient civilizations.

JANE AUSTEN (1775–1817) was an English novelist known primarily for her six major novels, which interpret, critique, and comment upon the British landed gentry at the end of the 18th century.

JAMES BALDWIN (1924–1987) was an American novelist, playwright, essayist, poet, and activist.

HENRY WARD BEECHER (1813–1887) was an American social reformer and speaker, known for his support of the abolition of slavery.

W. KAMAU BELL (1973–) is an American stand-up comic and television host.

SAUL BELLOW (1915–2005) was a Canadian American writer. He was awarded the Pulitzer Prize, the Nobel Prize for Literature, and the National Medal of Arts.

JILL BIDEN (1951–) is an American educator and the First Lady of the United States.

JON BING (1944–2014) was a Norwegian writer and law professor.

CHRIS BOHJALIAN (1962–) is an Armenian American novelist and the author of twenty novels, including *The Flight Attendant*.

ROBERTO BOLAÑO (1953–2003) was a Chilean novelist, short story writer, poet, and essayist best known for his novel *2666*.

LIBBA BRAY (1964–) is an American writer of young adult novels including the Gemma Doyle Trilogy, The Diviners series, and the novel *Going Bovine*.

ANATOLE BROYARD (1920–1990) was an American writer, literary critic, and editor who wrote for the *New York Times*.

LISA BU (UNKNOWN–) is a Chinese talk show producer, digital media content director, and computer programmer. She works at TED.

JACK CAVANAUGH (1952–) is an American author of Christian historical fiction. He is best known for his first series, American Family Portrait.

STEPHEN CHBOSKY (1970–) is an American novelist, screenwriter, and film director best known for *The Perks of Being a Wallflower*.

NOAM CHOMSKY (1928–) is an American linguist, philosopher, cognitive scientist, historian, social critic, and political activist.

CASSANDRA CLARE (1973–) is the pen name for Judith Lewis. An American YA author, Cassandra is best known for her best-selling series, The Mortal Instruments.

TA-NEHISI COATES (1975–) is an American author and journalist best known for his nonfiction book *Between the World and Me*.

STEPHEN COLBERT (1964–) is an American comedian, writer, producer, political commentator, actor, and television host.

MATSHONA DHLIWAYO (1982–) is a Canada-based Zimbabwean philosopher, entrepreneur, and author of books such as *The Art of Winning, Dinner with King Solomon,* and *Lalibela's Wise Man*.

JUNOT DÍAZ (1968–) is a Dominican American writer. He received the 2008 Pulitzer Prize for Fiction for his novel *The Brief Wondrous Life of Oscar Wao*.

ANNE DILLARD (1945–) is an American author who has published works of poetry, essays, prose, and literary criticism, as well as two novels and one memoir. Her 1974 work *Pilgrim at Tinker Creek* won the 1975 Pulitzer Prize for General Nonfiction.

WALT DISNEY (1901–1966) was an American storyteller, animator, and businessman who built an empire with a foundation of magic and very popular mouse.

CAROLE NELSON DOUGLAS (1944–) is an American writer best known for two popular mystery series, the Irene Adler Sherlockian suspense novels and the Midnight Louie mystery series.

RITA DOVE (1952–) is an American poet and essayist. She served as poet laureate of the United States from 1993 to 1995.

ALECHIA DOW (1985–) is an American author. Her books include *The Sound of Stars, The Kindred,* and *Sweet Stakes.*

STUART DYBEK (1942–) is an American author best known for three books of fiction: *I Sailed with Magellan, The Coast of Chicago,* and *Childhood and Other Neighborhoods.*

CLYDE EDGERTON (1944–) is an American author best known for his novels *Raney, Walking Across Egypt,* and *Killer Diller.*

ALBERT EINSTEIN (1879–1955) was a German-born theoretical physicist, widely acknowledged to be one of the greatest and most influential physicists of all time. Einstein is best known for developing the theory of relativity, but he also made important contributions to science and society.

CHARLES WILLIAM ELIOT (1834–1926) was an American academic who was president of Harvard University from 1869 to 1909, the longest term of any Harvard president.

EMILIO ESTEVEZ (1962–) is an American actor, film director, screenwriter, and producer.

JAMIE FORD (1968–) is an American author best known for his debut novel *Hotel on the Corner of Bitter and Sweet*.

TOBY FORWARD (1950–) is an English author best known for the Carnegie-nominated novel *Dragonborn,* the picture book *The Wolf's Story,* and the middle-grade novel *Traveling Backward.*

DOROTHEA BENTON FRANK (1951–2019) was an American novelist. Her novels include *Porch Lights* and *By Invitation Only.*

JEAN FRITZ (1915–2017) was an American children's writer best known for American biography and history.

CORNELIA FUNKE (1958–) is a German author of children's fiction, best known for the Ink Heart series.

NEIL GAIMAN (1960–) is an English author best known for the comic book series The Sandman and novels *Stardust, American Gods, Coraline,* and *The Graveyard Book.*

HENRY LOUIS GATES JR. (1950–) is an American literary critic, professor, historian, filmmaker, and public intellectual.

ROXANE GAY (1974–) is an American writer, professor, editor, and social commentator. Gay is best known for her essay collection *Bad Feminist.*

RUTH BADER GINSBURG (1933–2020) was an American lawyer and jurist who served as an associate justice of the Supreme Court of the United States.

MARY JO GODWIN (1949–) is an American library consultant, editor, and advocate for intellectual freedom.

JOHN GOODMAN (1952–) is an American actor.

GERMAINE GREER (1939–) is an Australian writer best known for her nonfiction book *The Female Eunuch.*

BJÖRK GUÐMUNDSDÓTTIR (1965–) is an Icelandic singer, songwriter, record producer, actress, and DJ.

MATT HAIG (1975–) is an English novelist and journalist. He has written both fiction and nonfiction for children and adults, often in the speculative fiction genre.

SUHEIR HAMMAD (1973–) is an American poet, author, performer, and political activist.

CARLA HAYDEN (1952–) is an American librarian and the fourteenth Librarian of Congress.

ERNEST HEMINGWAY (1899–1961) was an American novelist, short story writer, and journalist. His economical and understated style—which included his iceberg theory—had a strong influence on 20th-century fiction, while his adventurous lifestyle and public image brought him admiration from later generations.

AYAAN HIRSI ALI (1969–) is a Somali-born Dutch American activist, feminist, and author best known for her two autobiographies *Infidel* and *Nomad*.

JOHN JAKES (1932–) is an American writer best known for his North and South trilogy.

MARILYN JOHNSON (1954–) is an American writer best known for her nonfiction book *This Book Is Overdue! How Librarians and Cybrarians Can Save Us All.*

FRANZ KAFKA (1883–1924) was a German-language writer, who was born in Prague, Bohemia, now the Czech Republic.

STEPHEN KING (1947–) is a prolific American horror, thriller, and fantasy author who has written more than sixty-four novels and two hundred short stories.

BARBARA KINGSOLVER (1955–) is an American novelist, essayist, and poet. Her widely known works include *The Poisonwood Bible* and *Animal, Vegetable, Miracle*.

CARLA H. KRUEGER (2001–) is an English author of psychological thrillers, suspense novels, and dark crime comedies.

URSULA K. LE GUIN (1929–2018) was an American author best known for her works of speculative fiction the Earthsea fantasy series.

MADELEINE L'ENGLE (1918–2007) was an American writer of fiction, nonfiction, poetry, and young adult fiction, including *A Wrinkle in Time*.

DORIS LESSING (1919–2013) was a British Zimbabwean (Rhodesian) novelist. She was awarded the Nobel Prize in Literature in 2007.

GAIL CARSON LEVINE (1947–) is an American author of young adult books. Her first novel, *Ella Enchanted,* received a Newbery Honor in 1998.

C. S. LEWIS (1898–1963), born Clive Staples Lewis, was a renowned British writer and theologian, best known for *The Chronicles of Narnia.*

MANUEL LIMA (1978–) is a Portuguese American designer, author, and lecturer known for his work in information visualization and visual culture.

ALBERTO MANGUEL (1948–) is an Argentine Canadian anthologist, translator, essayist, and novelist. He is the author of *The Library at Night.*

ZIGGY MARLEY (1968–) is a Jamaican musician and philanthropist.

GEORGE R. R. MARTIN (1948–), full name George Raymond Richard Martin, is an American author best known for his legendary fantasy series, Game of Thrones.

ELIZABETH MCCRACKEN (1966–) is an American author best known for *The Giant's House,* a National Book Award finalist.

MARY MCNEAR (UNKNOWN–) is an American author best known for the Butternut Lake series.

MICHAEL MOORE (1954–) is an American documentary filmmaker, author, and activist.

CAITLIN MORAN (1975–) is an English journalist, author, and broadcaster.

CHRISTOPHER MORLEY (1890–1957) was the author of more than 100 novels, books of essays, and volumes of poetry.

TONI MORRISON (1931–2019) was an American novelist, essayist, and college professor. She won the 1988 Pulitzer Prize for *Beloved* and was awarded the 1993 Nobel Prize in Literature.

KATE MOSSE (1961–) is a British novelist, nonfiction and short story writer, and broadcaster. She is best known for her novel *Labyrinth*.

HARUKI MURAKAMI (1949–) is a Japanese writer. His most notable works include *A Wild Sheep Chase, Norwegian Wood, The Wind-Up Bird Chronicle,* and *Kafka on the Shore*.

VICKI MYRON (1947–) is an American author and librarian best known for her book *Dewey: The Small-Town Library Cat Who Touched the World,* written with Bret Witter.

AZAR NAFISI (1948–) is an Iranian American writer and professor of English literature. She is best known for *Reading Lolita in Tehran: A Memoir in Books.*

AMY NEFTZGER (UNKNOWN–) is an American author of fiction books for both adults and children.

PATRICK NESS (1971–) is a British American author, journalist, lecturer, and screenwriter best known for his young adult books including the Chaos Walking series and *A Monster Calls.*

CELESTE NG (1980–) is an American writer and novelist. She is best known for her novels *Everything I Never Told You, Little Fires Everywhere,* and *Our Missing Hearts.*

WILLIAM NICHOLSON (1948–) is a British screenwriter, playwright, and novelist. He received an Oscar nomination for two screenplays, *Shadowlands* and *Gladiator.*

JOYCE CAROL OATES (1938–) is an American writer. She is the author of fifty-eight novels, a number of plays and novellas, and many volumes of short stories, poetry, and nonfiction.

BARACK OBAMA (1961–) is an American politician who served as the forty-fourth president of the United States.

NNEDI OKORAFOR (1974–) is a Nigerian American writer of fantasy and science fiction for both children and adults.

SUSAN ORLEAN (1955–) is an American journalist and the best-selling author of *The Orchid Thief* and *The Library Book.*

L. J. M. OWEN (UNKNOWN–) is an Australian author, archaeologist, and librarian. Her crime novels include *The Great Divide* and three books in the Dr. Pimms archaeological mystery series.

JOHN PALFREY (1972–) is an American educator, scholar, and law professor.

ORHAN PAMUK (1952–) is a Turkish novelist, screenwriter, academic, and recipient of the 2006 Nobel Prize in Literature.

LINDA SUE PARK (1984–) is a Korean American children's novel and picture book author whose work *A Single Shard* won the Newbery Medal.

DOLLY PARTON (1946–) is an American singer, songwriter, multi-instrumentalist, actress, author, businesswoman, and humanitarian, known primarily for her work in country music.

NANCY PEARL (1945–) is an American librarian, author, and literary critic. She is best known for *Book Lust*.

LOUISE PENNY (1958–) is a Canadian author of mystery novels set in the Canadian province of Quebec.

PAULA POUNDSTONE (1959–) is an American stand-up comedian, author, actress, interviewer, and commentator.

PHILIP PULLMAN (1946–), also known as Sir Philip Nicholas Outram Pullman, is an English writer. His best-known books include the fantasy trilogy His Dark Materials.

ANNA QUINDLEN (1953–) is an American author, journalist, and opinion columnist. She is best known for her semi-autobiographical novel *One True Thing*.

DAN RATHER (1931–) is an American journalist and former national evening news anchor.

ISHMAEL REED (1938–) is an American poet, novelist, essayist, songwriter, composer, playwright, editor, and publisher known for his satirical works challenging American political culture. Perhaps his best-known work is *Mumbo Jumbo,* a sprawling and unorthodox novel set in 1920s New York.

MAARYA REHMAN (UNKNOWN–) is a public library specialist. She led the reopening of the British Council libraries in Lahore and Karachi as the director of libraries and outreach.

JASON REYNOLDS (1983–) is an American author of novels and poetry for young adult and middle-grade audiences.

KEITH RICHARDS (1943–) is an English musician, singer, and songwriter best known as the guitarist of the Rolling Stones.

THEODORE ROOSEVELT (1858–1919), often referred to as Teddy or by his initials, T. R., was an American politician, statesman, soldier, conservationist, naturalist, historian, and writer who served as the twenty-sixth president of the United States.

ROGER ROSENBLATT (1940–) is an American memoirist, essayist, and novelist. He was a longtime essayist for *Time* magazine and *PBS NewsHour.*

CARL T. ROWAN (1925–2000) was an American journalist, author, and government official.

SALMAN RUSHDIE (1947–) is a British Indian novelist and essayist.

PAM MUÑOZ RYAN (1951–) is an American writer who has written more than forty books for children and young adults, such as *Esperanza Rising*.

DR. SEUSS (1904–1991), real name Theodor Seuss Geisel, was an American children's author and cartoonist. His specific art style and aptitude for rhyme created an iconic collection of picture books that include but are not limited to *The Cat in the Hat, The Lorax,* and *Oh, The Places You'll Go.*

SIDNEY SHELDON (1917–2007) was an American writer, director, and producer. He is consistently cited as one of the top ten best-selling fiction writers of all time.

ROBIN SLOAN (1979–) is an American author best known for his debut novel, *Mr. Penumbra's 24-Hour Bookstore.*

ZADIE SMITH (1975–) is an English novelist, essayist, and short story writer best known for her debut novel *White Teeth.*

RICK STEVES (1955–) is an American travel writer, author, activist, and television personality.

TAYLOR SWIFT (1989–) is an American singer and songwriter known for her iconic pop titles that have reached international acclaim.

STUDS TERKEL (1912–2008) was an American author, historian, actor, and broadcaster. He won the Pulitzer Prize for *The Good War.*

ANGIE THOMAS (1988–) is an American young adult author best known for writing *The Hate U Give.*

BARBARA W. TUCHMAN (1912–1989) was an American historian and author. She won the Pulitzer Prize twice, for *The Guns of August* and *Stilwell and the American Experience in China.*

MARK TWAIN (1835–1910), also known as Samuel Langhorne Clemens, was an American writer and humorist. He is best known for his infamous tales *The Adventures of Tom Sawyer* and *The Adventures of Huckleberry Finn.*

SIMON VAN BOOY (1975–) is a British American author of works of fiction for adults, novels for children, and anthologies of philosophy.

KURT VONNEGUT (1922–2007) was an American writer. In a career spanning over fifty years, he published fourteen novels, three short story collections, five plays, and five nonfiction works.

ALICE WALKER (1944–) is an American novelist, short story writer, poet, and social activist. She won the 1983 Pulitzer Prize for Fiction for *The Color Purple*.

JO WALTON (1964–) is a Welsh Canadian fantasy and science fiction writer and poet. She is best known for her novels *Tooth and Claw, Ha'penny, Lifelode,* and *Among Others*.

LAUREN WARD (1970–) is an American singer and actress.

LINTON WEEKS (UNKNOWN–) is an American journalist and a national correspondent for NPR.

OSCAR WILDE (1854–1900), full name Oscar Fingal O'Flahertie Wills Wilde, was an Irish poet and playwright who became one of the most popular playwrights in London during the 1890s.

DOUG WILHELM (1952–) is an American author of seventeen books for young readers, including *Street of Storytellers*.

OPRAH WINFREY (1954–) is an American talk show host, television producer, actress, author, and philanthropist.

MALALA YOUSAFZAI (1997–) is a Pakistani activist for female education and the youngest Nobel Prize laureate.

CARLOS RUIZ ZAFÓN (1964–2020) was a Spanish novelist best known for his novel *La sombra del viento* (*The Shadow of the Wind*).

ROGER ZELAZNY (1937–1995) was an American poet and writer of fantasy and science fiction short stories and novels, best known for *The Chronicles of Amber*.

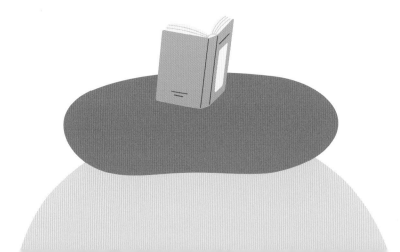

SOURCES

The gathering of quotes for this book would have been a more difficult process had it not been for the interviews and compilation work of others. The following newspapers, magazines, and websites were useful in curating content for this book.

ALA.org

American Libraries

The American Library Association YouTube Channel

AZ Quotes

Banned Book Weeks YouTube channel

Book Riot

Brain Pickings

The Chicago Public Library Foundation

Goodreads

Granta

The Guardian

Halifax Public Libraries' website

Huff Post

ilovelibraries.org

The New York Public Library Blog

New York Times

New Yorker

NPR.org

Patriot Ledger

Psychology Today

Scholastic.com

Seattle Times

TED.com

Washington Post

Wikiquote

About the ALA

The American Library Association (ALA) is the foremost national organization providing resources to inspire library and information professionals to transform their communities through essential programs and services. ALA condemns censorship and works to ensure free access to information. Every year, ALA's Office for Intellectual Freedom (OIF) compiles a list of the Top 10 Most Challenged Books to inform the public about censorship in libraries and schools. The lists are based on information from media stories and voluntary reports sent to OIF from communities across the United States. In addition, OIF hosts Banned Books Week, an annual event typically held the last week of September that highlights the benefits of free and open access to information and draws attention to censorship attempts.

Learn more about how you can support the freedom to read and stay connected to what's going on in libraries at ilovelibraries.org.